Tales
Historic Dorset

by Robert Westwood

Inspiring Places Publishing
2 Down Lodge Close
Alderholt
Fordingbridge
SP6 3JA

ISBN 978-0-9928073-4-4

www.inspiringplaces.co.uk

Contents:

Introduction

Dorset has always been a rural, agricultural land, still with no city or motorway, yet it has featured in many defining episodes of British history. Roman, Saxon, Viking and Norman armies have all marched across its lovely landscape and civil war battles have been fought here. Its ports have played a part in world history, including the last world war when over half a million soldiers embarked for France from Weymouth alone.

Rather than giving a complete history of the county, this book provides glimpses into its colourful and fascinating past and of the people and places associated. Exploring Dorset's beautiful landscape with a little of this knowledge can be a rewarding experience. The book is divided into sections detailing interesting historical episodes centred on particular areas throughout the county but with some sections devoted to particular themes that involved a number of different areas, for example, the Civil War.

Reminders of its rich history are everywhere in Dorset. Castles, abbeys, great houses and ancient monuments draw tourists from all over the world. As you explore this lovely county this guide will help you appreciate its wonderful heritage.

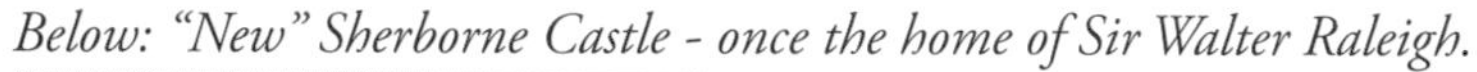

Below: "New" Sherborne Castle - once the home of Sir Walter Raleigh.

Lyme Regis

The harbour at Lyme Regis is one of the most instantly recognisable of any on the south coast of England. The famous curved wall of the Cobb has featured in films, on television and in many atmospheric photographs. This artificial harbour was first mentioned in the thirteenth century; there had previously been no safe haven for shipping between Exeter and Weymouth. The Saxon king Cynewulf had granted land here to the monks of Sherborne and also a licence to make salt. In 1284 the town received a Royal Charter from Edward I and Regis was added to the name.

The labours of those who built and continually repaired the Cobb ensured Lyme became a busy and profitable port and it is perhaps no surprise that a number of famous names are associated with the town. Its medieval inhabitants would have had no idea that the treasures in its cliffs would guarantee Lyme's fame long after it had ceased to be an important trading post.

Admiral Sir George Somers was born in Lyme Regis in 1544. He had an illustrious career, helping to see off the Spanish Armada, becoming an MP and mayor of the port and founding the London Virginia Company. In 1609 he was shipwrecked off Bermuda on his way to Virginia and claimed the island for Britain; it became the first loyal Crown colony.

Above: The Cobb at Lyme Regis.

Above: The 'Ammonite Pavement' on Monmouth Beach, Lyme Regis.

One unfortunate famous visitor to Lyme Regis has given his name to the beach west of the Cobb. James, Duke of Monmouth, landed here in 1685 with 400 men at the start of his ill-fated expedition to take the throne from the Catholic James II. Monmouth was a Protestant and the illegitimate son of Charles II. He had a reputation as a clever and skilful soldier and his force had soon swelled to 6000 men. However, the royal army, although smaller, was much more experienced and better trained and Monmouth was defeated at the Battle of Sedgemoor in Somerset. The infamous Judge Jeffries was selected to oversee the trials of the rebels and following a short hearing at Lyme had twelve men hanged on Monmouth Beach.

A number of celebrated women are associated with the town; Jane Austen was another famous visitor to Lyme in 1803 and 1804. She fell in love with the area and the town and Cobb featured in her novel *Persuasion*. Eleanor Coade of Lyme Regis was an enterprising woman; around 1770 she perfected the recipe for an artificial or manufactured stone that was particularly hard wearing and resistant to erosion. Coade Stone was used extensively for statues and mouldings. The facade of Belmont House, her home in Lyme Regis, is made out of the stone. A large amount of the stone was used in the refurbishment of Buckingham Palace.

Perhaps the most famous woman associated with Lyme Regis is the fossil hunter Mary Anning. However, Lyme Regis Museum is also known as the Philpot Museum after the three Philpot sisters who gathered an extensive fossil collection from the local area in the early nineteenth century. Elizabeth

Philpot became well known as an expert on fossil fish and was consulted by some of the leading geologists of the time. She befriended a young Mary Anning, despite a considerable age difference and the fact that Mary was from a less priviliged background. It was Elizabeth who encouraged Mary to study geology and science, and the two collected many fossils together.

The Natural History Museum's website calls Mary Anning "the greatest fossil collector ever known". Born in 1799 to a poor family, Mary was one of two out of ten children to survive. Her father was a carpenter who made some extra money by selling fossils in a small shop. When he died, aged forty-four, Mary continued the business and her reputation as an expert collector soon grew. Mary unearthed the first complete skeleton of an ichthyosaur and the first two skeletons of a plesiosaur. Many of her finds are now housed in the Natural History Museum. She, too, was consulted by eminent geologists and scientists and was even granted an annuity by the Geological Association. The Royal Society has named Mary Anning as third in the list of women who have most influenced the history of science. One interesting discovery of Mary's is related to a very common fossil. The bullet shaped cones of belemnites are found in their thousands. These creatures are related to the squid and the two hundred million year old ink from their fossilised ink sacs can be revivified and used to produce drawings. Mary Anning only left Lyme Regis once for a short trip to London and died, aged forty-seven from breast cancer.

Bridport

Bridport was once one of Dorset's most important towns; in Saxon times it was a fortified "burh", one of four developed by Alfred the Great as defence against the Danes. It may not seem like it now but Bridport, as the name suggests, was also a port and flat bottomed boats could reach the town at high tide in the thirteenth century. The silting of the River Brit was one of the factors that led to the town's major industry – rope and net making. The climate and rich alluvial soils are perfect for growing flax and hemp. The first written records of Bridport's rope making industry date from the twelfth century, but it had certainly been going on for hundreds of years before then. For many years the main customer for ropes was the Navy; in 1211 King John ordered such quantities of hemp thread for the imminent war with France that for two years the work had to go on twenty-four hours a day. Later on when the Navy found it cheaper to spin rope nearer to their dockyards, the Bridport industry was saved by the increased demand caused by the growth of the East India Company and the fishing industry of Newfoundland. Although most of Bridport's buildings date from the eighteenth century onwards, the rope

Above: The busy working harbour at West Bay.

making industry has left its mark in the many long, narrow gardens and wide streets which were necessary for spinning and drying the rope respectively. Although the industry became more centralised in the nineteenth century with manufacturing concentrated in mills, it was many years before out workers were not used. Today the firm started by Jacob Gundry in 1665 is still making nets and ropes for a wide variety of uses; the goal nets for the 1966 World Cup final were made in Bridport! On a more sinister note, when a criminal met his end on the gallows he was said to have been "stabbed by a Bridport dagger" as the rope would inevitably have been made there.

Bridport's harbour was originally on the estuary of the River Brit and from the fourteenth to the eighteenth century varied in its use and the facilities it offered. In the nineteenth century it was decided to create a larger harbour basin with longer entrance piers. Throughout the twentieth century storm damage was frequently repaired and in 2001 a decision was taken to build a west pier and refurbish the east pier. The "Jurassic Pier" opened in 2004 and is a great place to view the spectacular East Cliffs. Bridport Harbour was only renamed West Bay in the late nineteenth century and today is a thriving harbour for fishing vessels and leisure craft. West Bay has been used as a location in a number of television and film productions, including the television drama "Broadchurch" and the 2015 film version of Thomas Hardy's "Far From the Madding Crowd".

Abbotsbury

Abbotsbury is a delightful village built with the local golden Jurassic limestone. An abbey here was founded in the eleventh century by a thegn of King Canute called Orc. Although Canute was a "heathen", it seems Orc was Christian and, having been granted lands at Abbotsbury by the king, founded a Benedictine monastery, probably on the site of the ancient church of St Peter. He retained the support of Edward the Confessor after Canute and was granted more land along the sea shore. Orc left everything to the church when he died, a bequest that was confirmed by William the Conqueror; thereafter the Abbey of St Peter continued to grow and prosper. Although it too suffered during the Black Death, by the fifteenth century it had recovered and was expanding, evidenced by the building of the great tithe barn and St Catherine's Chapel. These two buildings survived the Dissolution of the Monasteries by Henry VIII probably because of their usefulness, the latter as a lookout and marker for shipping. The famous Swannery was founded by the early monks

Above: The meagre remains of the old abbey.
Below: Abbotsbury Church. Opposite page: The Fleet.

who farmed the swans for food; the Fleet lagoon with its shallow, brackish water is an ideal nesting ground.

Much of Abbotsbury's turbulent history is centred around the Fleet. It provided a safe haven for Saxon and Viking raiders who ravaged the local area and centuries later was found by local smugglers to be a very convenient place for storing and transporting contraband. More recently it provided the setting for the testing of a secret weapon, Barnes Wallis's famous bouncing bomb used in the Dambusters raid. Being a long stretch of very shallow water it was ideal for dropping and recovering the bombs afterwards. The first tests were carried out on the Fleet in late 1942 and early 1943. Langton Herring, the charming village behind the Fleet is known as a "doubly thankful" village; all of its men and women who went to the two world wars came home safely, one of only fourteen such villages nation wide.

One of the most dramatic events in the history of the Fleet began on the evening of November 22nd 1824. This was the great storm which wreaked havoc along the south coast. Weymouth's harbour was all but destroyed and the Cobb at Lyme Regis severely damaged. The village of Fleet, tucked in behind Chesil Beach might have expected some protection from the worst of the waves but in the early hours of the morning one freak wave breached Chesil Beach and wrecked the village. In what remains of the old church at East Fleet, it records the depth of water as thirty feet. Fishing boats were carried right over Chesil Beach and there was widespread flooding of the surrounding area. It has been suggested that this wave was a "meteorological tsunami" caused by a chance combination of weather conditions.

The Flight of Charles II

The Civil War did not end with the execution of Charles I in 1649. In 1650 the Scottish Presbyterians invited his son in exile to Scotland, with the aim of helping him regain the throne. He accepted the invitation against the advice of his most trusted confidants and a wholly unsuccessful campaign ended in defeat at the Battle of Worcester in 1651. Paradoxically, the events of the following weeks would forever enhance the reputation of the future Charles II.

The story of Charles' flight from Worcester has passed into folklore as a classic tale of royalty disguised among ordinary people. He faced almost constant danger but showed courage, fortitude and presence of mind to evade capture and eventually escape to France. Many days of this much recounted adventure were spent in Dorset, where he was given shelter by Colonel Francis Wyndham, a staunch Royalist hero of the Civil War, who owned the manor at Trent near Sherborne.

Together, Wyndham and Charles' supporters formulated a plan; they found a captain at Lyme Regis willing to take them to France. They would go down to Charmouth the previous day and stay at an inn, leaving in the middle of the night. Charles would pretend to be the manservant to a couple planning to elope. The landlady of the inn loved the story and promised to tell no one. It was a brave but risky plan – news of a reward for the capture of Charles had recently been publicised and Lyme Regis would be packed with people attending a fair. A messenger was meant to tell the party when to leave but when he didn't arrive the royal party became nervous and decided to leave. Charles and Colonel Wyndham left for Bridport and rented a room at the best inn. The town was full of troops and Charles, still acting the manservant, led the horses to the stable which was already crowded with soldiers. Shortly after the hostler of the inn

Previous page: Trent church next to the house where Charles hid. Its bells were once rung to celebrate his capture while he was staying there! Above left and right: Plaques commemorating his hiding places, left at Broadwindsor and right Charmouth, a former inn where Catherine of Aragon also once stayed.

announced that he thought he recognised Charles' face and it says a lot about his nerve that he came through these tricky situations.

What the royal party did not know was that the hostler at Charmouth had become suspicious and raised the alarm. Charles and his supporters calmly left their lodging in the morning taking the road to Dorchester. After a short while they changed their minds and took a small lane back in the direction of Trent. Five minutes later the chasing soldiers galloped past on their way to Dorchester! A small plaque now marks the spot where a spur of the moment decision saved the king's life. The party became hopelessly lost and stumbled upon the village of Broadwindsor. Here they found an inn owned by a loyal Royalist who agreed to let them use the top room. As they were settling down for what they hoped would be a peaceful night a party of Commonwealth soldiers arrived at the inn. Luck was on their side again; in the middle of the night one of the camp followers gave birth and there was much concern amongst the villagers that the party would leave the child behind. After much heated discussion the soldiers were forced to leave early in the morning – the interests of the mother and child apparently counted for little.

Eventually Charles and his party reached the safety of Trent, still unaware of why the ship in Lyme Regis had failed to take them to France. It turns out that the captain of the ship had told his wife about the "runaway lovers" and, perhaps being less gullible, had become suspicious and begged him not to go. He refused but she took an opportunity to lock him in his room and did not let him out until the morning!

Charles finally did get a boat to France from Shoreham in Sussex and never forgot his adventures in Dorset, returning several times to visit and reward the people who had helped him.

Weymouth

Between 1180 and 1280 Dorset, and much of the south of England, experienced a relative golden age. The climate had entered a warm phase at the beginning of the twelfth century, agriculture had prospered and the population of England had risen to nearly six million, a figure not reached again until the eighteenth century. Thriving market towns, rich abbeys and prosperous manors were to be found all over Dorset.

Things began to change at the start of the fourteenth century; the climate entered a cooler cycle and huge volcanic eruptions in Indonesia contributed to two terrible summers in 1316 and 1317. There was widespread famine. Then, on the 25th June 1348 a small merchant ship docked at Melcombe Regis (now part of Weymouth) and initiated a chain of events that would devastate the population of Dorset and England. It is generally accepted that the ship's rats were infected with fleas that carried the bacteria responsible for bubonic plague and that people became infected when bitten. Today a plaque at 7, Custom House Quay commemorates this terrible event. Within four days the first deaths from the disease occurred in the port and the plague soon spread to neighbouring villages. West Chickerell became the first Dorset village to lose its priest and many more were to follow as the clergy nursed the sick and dying. Portland was particularly badly affected and quarries were abandoned. In 1352 Edward III issued orders restricting the movement of people there.

In 2007 evidence from the Dorset town of Gillingham cast doubt on the assumption that the Pestilence (the name Black Death was not used until much later) was entirely due to bubonic plague. Court records show that most of the deaths there happened during the winter months, a time when the fleas should have been dormant. It may be that, in a population already weakened by famine, other diseases, possibly viral, also took hold. Whatever the cause, about forty to fifty per cent of England's population perished and Dorset was one of the worst hit areas.

The twin ports Melcombe Regis, north of the river, and Weymouth, south of the river, survived the plague and prospered again. There developed a bitter rivalry between the two, ending in 1571 when a Royal Charter granted by Elizabeth I sensibly united them as the Borough of Weymouth and Melcombe Regis. In 1588 six ships from the port contributed to the defeat of the Spanish Armada. A little over two hundred years later a naval captain from nearby Portesham played a part in saving the country again from the threat of invasion. Thomas Masterman Hardy was born in 1769 at Kingston

Above: The old harbour at Weymouth. The estuary of the River Wey originally divided the towns of Melcombe Regis (far side of the river) and Weymouth.

Russell House at Long Bredy and later lived at Portesham House. He had an illustrious career in the Royal Navy and was Nelson's Flag Captain on HMS Victory during the Battle of Trafalgar. He later rose to the rank of First Lord of the Admiralty and Vice Admiral. In 1844 the Hardy Monument on Black Down was erected by public subscription in his honour. Standing twenty-two metres tall it commands a wonderful view point and was specifically placed there so it could be used as a navigation aid by shipping. Its shape is meant to resemble a spyglass that Hardy would have used on board ship. Weymouth played its part during the Second World War when over half a million men embarked from the port to France for, and following, the invasion of Normandy.

The waters around Portland Bill can be treacherous and many ships have come to grief here. In February 1805, the year of Trafalgar, the East Indiaman, "Earl of Abergavenny" sank in a storm off Portland Bill and two hundred and sixty-one people lost their lives, including the captain, John Wordsworth, brother of William. The event inspired William to write "Elegiac Stanzas". John Wordsworth is buried, along with many of the other victims, in the graveyard of All Saints Church, Wyke Regis.

The Isle of Portland

Stone has been quarried on Portland since Roman times but the industry really developed in the seventeenth century, particularly after Sir Christopher Wren chose Portland Stone for the rebuilding of St Paul's Cathedral. On Portland the thick layers of Jurassic limestone slope gently down towards the sea on the southern side of the isle; this greatly facilitated the transport of the stone by ship. The zenith of the quarrying industry was in the nineteenth century when the coming of the railway meant stone could be transported inland and steam powered machinery was available. The 1851 census showed that of a male population of 2143 there were 480 quarrymen and 33 stonemasons.

Portland Castle, built in 1539 was one of a string of fortifications built along the south coast by Henry VIII to guard against a possible invasion from France and Spain. It is one of the best examples of these castles and Dorset's only intact medieval castle. Funded by the confiscations during the Dissolution of the Monasteries, the castle, with its sister fortification at Sandsfoot, Weymouth, also provided protection from pirates. The Channel had become a very important trading route and Portland Harbour was a key refuge for merchant ships which became prey to French privateers. Although very effective in its role of reducing piracy, in 1544 the brother of the castle's governor, George Strangways, was himself a pirate and it is reported that the castle was used to store his loot! The main military action the castle saw was

Below: The gateway to Portland Castle with the coat of arms of Charles II.

Above: Portland Bill lighthouse is surrounded by old quarry workings. Right: Portland Museum.

during the Civil War (see page 18) when, as a Royalist stronghold, it came under siege several times by the Parliamentarians.

Portland Museum at Church Ope Cove, housed in two pretty cottages, tells the story of the island's quarrying, its maritime history, geology and people. It was founded in 1930 by Marie Stopes, scientist and pioneer of birth control. She lived in one of the cottages for a while as well as the old lighthouse.

Between 1849 and 1872 the breakwaters of Portland Harbour were constructed. This was one of Britain's greatest government engineering projects and used labour from the nearby prison. The breakwaters were built using Portland Stone and enclosed one of the world's largest man made harbours. Also at this time the Verne Citadel, the East Weare Battery and the present Nothe Fort were constructed. These new defences relieved the castle of its defensive duties but it returned to military use during both world wars. In World War I a Royal Navy air station flew anti-submarine missions from beside the castle while in World War II it was the temporary home to many British and American servicemen in the months before D-Day.

The Civil War in Dorset

Stories from the English Civil War (1642 to 1651) are to be found in many towns and villages all over the British Isles. Some of these stories are romantic or humorous, and populated by dashing figures in colourful costumes. However, it is worth remembering what a violent and brutal conflict this was. It has been estimated that one in ten of the adult male population died in this war; three times the proportion of men killed in World War I. At least one hundred thousand people died from war related disease. Dorset suffered badly and our first story relates to the stark facts mentioned above.

There were few major battles in the Civil War, but many minor skirmishes and sieges. The armies of both sides continually marched through the countryside taking what they needed from the local area. The soldiers were badly paid, if at all, discipline was often weak and the hardships inflicted on rural populations were considerable. Small scale uprisings and attacks on soldiers became more frequent and during the winter of 1644-1645 a more general movement of rebellion was beginning to emerge. Groups known as "Clubmen" were organised in a number of counties, often by local clergy. These men were not on either side of the conflict but were tired of the constant ravaging of their communities and declared themselves opposed to both armies. They armed themselves with anything available, a practice that clearly led to their name. Dorset had particularly suffered from the demands

Above: Hambledon Hill, Iron Age hillfort and scene of the last stand of the Dorset Clubmen.

Above: Badbury Rings - another hillfort used by the Dorset Clubmen.

of the armies of both sides and in May 1645 around four thousand Clubmen gathered at Badbury Rings and organised groups to seize army plunderers. This was probably the most effective thing they could do to protect their area; meeting trained troops head on in battle would not have been feasible. Later in the summer the Clubmen began to plot to put an end to the siege of Sherborne which was held by a small Royalist garrison. General Fairfax, in charge of the Parliamentarians, captured a band of Clubmen at Shaftesbury but despite his assurances that plundering by his soldiers would be severely punished, the Clubmen continued to gather and pose a threat. In August 1645 between two and four thousand Clubmen assembled on Hambledon Hill and Oliver Cromwell was sent with around one thousand dragoons to sort the matter out.

Twice Cromwell sent a small party of dragoons to negotiate and get the Clubmen to lay down their arms. Both times they were met with threats. Eventually Cromwell sent more troops who threatened to charge the Clubmen but told them that no harm would be done to them if they laid down their arms. The Clubmen opened fire, killing two dragoons. One story says that a traitor had taken a party of Cromwell's soldiers through another entrance of the Iron Age hillfort, but whatever the truth of this it seems the Clubmen soon scattered when the dragoons charged. Around sixty were killed and many taken prisoner. Cromwell led the prisoners to the church at Shroton at the foot of the hill and locked them up there overnight. It is reported that he gave them a stern lecture the following morning before sending the majority back to their homes. Those killed were buried in a mass grave in the churchyard.

At the start of the Civil War Dorset was largely in the hands of the forces of Parliament, in particular important ports like Lyme Regis and Weymouth. During the war the Royalists, at times, made significant gains and there were a number of bitter conflicts and sieges in and around Dorset's ancient towns.

In 1644 Lyme Regis was controlled by Parliament and in April of that year Prince Maurice marched on the town with a Royalist army some six thousand strong. He deployed his men in an arc around the town and for two months a bitter siege raged. The defenders survived artillery bombardments, fire arrows and two attempts to storm the town before Prince Maurice finally withdrew after hearing Parliamentarian reinforcements were on the way.

Most major engagements during the Civil War were either sieges or battles in open territory; Weymouth was unusual in that it was the scene of bitter street fighting in February 1645. It had been held by Parliament for some time with a relatively small garrison. A plot known as the "Crabchurch Conspiracy" was hatched by Royalists in Weymouth. Some of the king's forces in Portland, reinforced by islanders would seize the twin forts of Chapel and Nothe and simultaneously a group of Royalists in the town would open the gates to let in the army under Sir Lewis Dyve. Things did not quite go according to plan, the forts were seized but the army was not there. In the following days however, Sir Lewis did arrive and also another four and a half thousand men under Lord Goring. The Parliamentarians were heavily outnumbered; bitter fighting in the streets ensued for many days. In the end the Parliamentarians hung on and retained the town, thanks in no small way to the gallantry and cunning of an officer called Thomas Sydenham, the younger brother of the town's Governor.

The Sydenham family lived in the manor at Wynford Eagle, north-west of Dorchester. All the sons of the family took up arms for Parliament and Francis Sydenham became the Governor of Weymouth. The father, William was captured by Royalists who also murdered his wife, Mary, on the doorstep of their manor home. In November 1644 Major Francis Sydenham spotted the man who had killed his mother at Poole. Together with a small party of cavalrymen, he charged at the Royalist group and chased them all the way to Dorchester. Finally, Major Francis caught up with his mother's murderer, shot him and trampled him with his horse. Francis was later killed at the siege of Weymouth.

One of the most well known episodes in the Civil War is the siege of Corfe Castle. Sir John Bankes, the Attorney General, had bought the castle in 1634. He remained loyal to the king and in 1643 the castle was besieged. Sir John was with the king in Oxford and it was left to his wife, Lady Bankes, to organise the defence. She did this with such skill that the castle held out for six weeks until relieved by a force under Lord Caernarvon. However, by December 1645 most of the West Country was in Parliamentary hands and a renewed effort to take the castle was made. Sir John had died in 1644 and so it was left to Lady Bankes again to hold the castle. Once more the defence held out for weeks until in February 1646 an officer named Colonel Pitman betrayed the defenders by letting the attackers into the castle; he had been pretending to negotiate an exchange of prisoners. There was no option but to surrender. Lady Bankes had so impressed by her skill and courage that she was allowed to leave with her honour intact. The ancient defences of the castle had proved such an obstacle that it was 'slighted', gunpowder was used to bring down the walls. The ruins you see today are the result of this. After the Restoration the castle was returned to the Bankes family who, unable to use it again, built a splendid new home at Kingston Lacy.

Many smaller clashes took place during the Civil War as the Parliamentarians attacked isolated pockets of Royalist support. One such pocket was Abbotsbury where the garrison was commanded by Sir James Strangways. In 1644 it was attacked and some fierce fighting followed. The fighting even spread to the church; look inside at the pulpit and you will see a number of holes made by musket balls during the encounter. The village was finally taken and another Royalist outpost removed.

Below left: The manor house at Wynford Eagle, scene of the murder of Mary Sydenham. Right: Bullet hole in the pulpit of the church at Abbotsbury.

Sherborne

Saint Aldhelm was born around 639 AD in Wessex, probably to a member of the royal family. He spent his early years at Malmesbury but later moved to study at the Abbey of St Augustine in Canterbury. His reputation as a scholar quickly grew and he was also a fine musician. He moved back to Malmesbury where he was appointed abbot in 675. He introduced Benedictine rule there and is thought to have been the first Anglo-Saxon to write in Latin verse. In 705 the See of Sherborne was created and Aldhelm became its first bishop. He is said to have sung and played in public places to attract attention to his Christian message. This was a time when the Celtic kingdom of Dumnonia still existed in Devon and Cornwall. Aldhelm wrote to the King of Dumnonia in an attempt to gain his agreement on the calculation of Easter and his letter gives a fascinating insight into relations between the Saxons and the Britons they had replaced. Aldhelm died in 709, was buried in Malmesbury Abbey and soon venerated as a saint. He was a tireless evangelist and is thought to have set up a number of churches around Dorset; St Aldhelm's Chapel on St Aldhelm's Head was probably one of these although the present building is clearly much later.

Sherborne Abbey is now a parish church. After the bishopric was moved to Old Sarum in 1075 it became an abbey until the Dissolution of the Monasteries in 1539 when it was bought by the people of Sherborne for

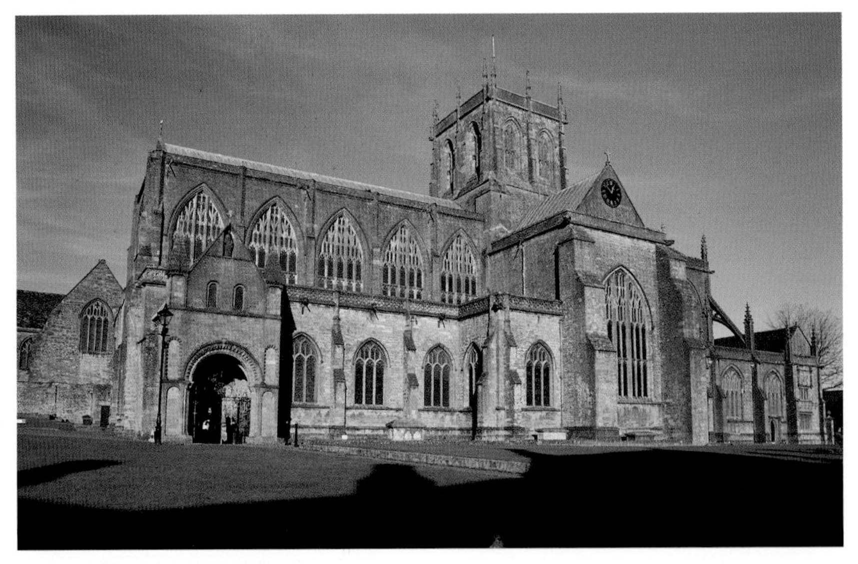

Above: Sherborne Abbey.

Above left: The wonderful fan vaulting in the nave of Sherborne Abbey, carved out of the local Jurassic Ham Stone. Right: A statue of St Aldhelm in the abbey.

their church. The present building mostly dates from the fifteenth century and is constructed from the local, golden Jurassic limestone known as Ham Stone. It has become widely famous for the magnificent fan vaulting of the choir and nave. The North Choir Aisle is thought to contain the tombs of Aethelbald and Ethelbert, elder brothers of Alfred the Great. The school next to the abbey was also founded in 705 and has many distinguished names among its past pupils, including David Cornwall (John Le Carre), Cecil Day Lewis, Jeremy Irons, Chris Martin and Alan Turing.

Another Saxon connection with Sherborne involves St Juthwara who lived in the sixth century in the nearby village of Halstock. Legend has it that a jealous stepmother falsely implied to Juthwara's brother that she was pregnant. Fearing dishonour to the family, he immediately struck off the pious girl's head. A spring gushed from the spot and Juthwara picked up her head and carried it to the church. The poor girl had apparently been set up by her stepmother's recommendation that she put soft cheeses to her chest to ease a pain. Her remains were revered in Sherborne Abbey until the Dissolution and a depiction of her can still be seen in the Great East Window.

Sherborne's Castles

Sherborne has two, neighbouring castles set in beautiful parkland on the edge of the town. Old Sherborne Castle was built in the twelfth century for Roger de Caen, Bishop of Salisbury and chancellor to King Henry I. When Roger switched sides to Matilda in the civil war known as "the Anarchy", the castle was besieged and taken by King Stephen. It was still owned by the Crown during the reign of Elizabeth I, and it was at this time that the castle fell into the hands of its most famous custodian, Sir Walter Raleigh. Raleigh had apparently fallen in love with the castle and its setting after passing it on the way to Plymouth from London. He persuaded the queen to grant him the lease in 1592 but despite its romantic setting Raleigh found the castle uninhabitable. Undeterred, he had the "new" castle built next door on the site of the old hunting lodge and lived there for about ten years. Rendering of the outside walls was the latest fashion at the time. The gardens were later remodelled by Capability Brown who also created the lake. The daring adventurer eventually fell out of favour with the queen and famously met his end in the Tower of London; his ghost is said to still wander the grounds. Sherborne Castle was acquired by the diplomat Sir John Digby in 1617 and is still the home of the Wingfield Digby family.

Above: "New" Sherborne Castle built on the instructions of Sir Walter Raleigh has delightful grounds and gardens to explore.

Left: The remains of the old castle at Sherborne are maintained by English Heritage.

Shaftesbury

Situated on the edge of the great Chalk escarpment overlooking the Vale of Blackmore, Shaftesbury was one of the defensive "burhs" created in 880 AD by Alfred the Great in response to the Viking threat. Eight years later he founded the abbey and installed his daughter Aethelgifu as abbess. After the body of King Edward the Martyr was brought here following his murder at Corfe Castle, Shaftesbury Abbey became one of the richest and most important in the country. Edward was canonised in 1008 and pilgrims flocked to his shrine. The abbey was a favourite of King Canute; he died here in 1035 and although his burial casket remains in Winchester Cathedral, it is said his heart was buried in Shaftesbury. The "Shaftesbury Bowl", now in the museum at Winchester Cathedral, is a glass bowl discovered under the high altar in Shaftesbury Abbey in the late nineteenth century that may have contained Canute's heart.

Edward's remains were hidden at the time of the Dissolution but in 1931 a casket was discovered during archaeological excavations that possibly contained his remains. Later examination showed that the remains were from a man who had died in the manner Edward had. The owner of the site wanted the remains to go to a church where they would be recognised as those of a saint, eventually deciding on the Russian Orthodox Church who venerated some of the early English kings because of their religious reforms. Others wanted the remains returned to Shaftesbury and for many years they were kept in a bank vault in Woking. Eventually they were given to the care of the St Edward the Martyr Orthodox Brotherhood in Brookwood, Surrey in whose church they now rest.

The Blackmore Vale from Shaftesbury

Dorchester

Dorset's county town came into being as a Roman settlement around 60 AD. Known as Durnovaria, it soon developed into an important administrative and trading centre. What happened to it after the Romans left is not certain but it was only a very small town at the time of the Norman Conquest, although it was one of four Dorset boroughs recorded in the Domesday survey. Between 1068 and 1071 rebellions in the north and west were brutally put down by King William and the Domesday Book records a sad picture of the devastation caused by the Norman army as it marched west. In 1066 Dorchester was recorded as having 172 houses, but by 1086 only 88, the rest having been destroyed. The Normans built a wooden castle there and throughout the medieval era Dorchester remained a small market town, its prosperity based on the wool industry until the eighteenth century when brewing took over.

In the 1720s Daniel Defoe went on a tour of England and later wrote about his experiences. He liked Dorchester very much; he found the town pleasant with broad streets, but it was the people who really impressed him. He wrote, "there is good company and a good deal of it; a man that coveted a retreat in this world might as agreeably spend his time, and as well in Dorchester, as in any town I know in England".

Above: Dorchester remains a pleasant, agreeable place.

Above: Cottages in Milton Abbas, an early example of town (or village) planning.
Left: Milton Abbey viewed from St Catherine's Chapel. The abbey is now in the grounds of Milton Abbey School and is open to visitors.

Milton Abbas

Eleven miles north-east of Dorchester lies the picturesque village of Milton Abbas, whose charm belies its dramatic and sorrowful origin. It was built in 1773 by Joseph Damer, the 1st Earl of Dorchester. He was a wealthy landowner who had bought Milton Abbey with plans to develop and build a grand residence. The small town of Middleton had grown up around the abbey and Lord Milton, as he was known, did not much like his view spoiled by the dwellings of the locals. He consequently had the whole town demolished and a new village constructed in a nearby wooded valley – well out of sight. The mostly identical cottages were originally split into two dwellings and were much more crowded than they are now. The grounds of the earl's new home were landscaped by Capability Brown.

Milton Abbey was founded by King Athelstan in 933 in memory of his brother Edwin who had drowned at sea, an event for which Athelstan may have been responsible. The abbey prospered until the Dissolution in 1539, despite a fire in 1309 which destroyed the medieval church. The present church reached its current size around 1400 but was never finished. After the Dissolution the abbey was bought by Sir John Tregonwell whose great grandson, also John Tregonwell, features in an interesting story concerning the abbey. In 1605, as a child, he reportedly fell from the roof but was saved by his pantaloons which billowed out and slowed his fall.

Cerne Abbas

The quaint and ancient settlement of Cerne Abbas is widely known as the location of a one hundred and eighty feet high chalk figure of a naked giant cut into a hillside to the north of the village. The origin of this curious figure is still disputed; some think it may date from Roman times as it appears to be a caricature of Hercules, or possibly a Celtic god. However, there is no written record of the giant before 1694 and many now believe it dates from the seventeenth century and may represent a parody of Oliver Cromwell who was sometimes mockingly called "England's Hercules" by his enemies. Whatever its origins it was, perhaps, inevitable that folklore would develop around it, particularly associations with fertility! It has been claimed that couples who wish to conceive should spend the night on the giant and locals used to erect a maypole on the hill where childless couples would dance to promote fertility. Each year at dawn on Mayday, members of the Wessex Morris Men dance at the Iron Age earthwork just above the giant. It is an engaging and atmospheric experience for those who can make the effort to get up early and be there.

Many visitors to Cerne Abbas miss its other great treasures, the charming remains of what was once a prosperous Benedictine abbey and the wonderfully tranquil Silver Well. The abbey was founded in the tenth century and was both raided and later endowed by King Canute. The abbey buildings were largely demolished following the Dissolution but the Abbot's Porch and the Guest House remain. Although privately owned, they can be viewed. Nearby at one end of the graveyard lies the Silver Well. Sometimes known as St Augustine's Well because of a local legend that it sprang from the saint's staff during a visit here; its probable, real history is much more interesting. The spring is said to be at the site of a hermitage occupied by St Edwold, the brother of St Edmund the Martyr, king of East Anglia. Edwold had become disillusioned by constant warfare and, following the death of his brother at the hands of the Vikings, had a vision of the well. He set off in search of it and on coming to Cerne Abbas he gave silver pennies to shepherds in return for food and water. They brought him to the well. A local superstition says that it is beneficial to dip new born babies in it as the first rays of the sun touch the water. It is a lovely, peaceful spot, ideal for quiet reflection.

Main picture, right: The Abbot's Porch at Cerne Abbas, dating from the fourteenth century.
Inset: The Silver Well in a corner of the nearby churchyard.

The Isle of Purbeck

The Isle of Purbeck has a beauty and heritage to match any part of England. Although not really an island it is washed by the sea on three sides. Its southern coast of rugged limestone cliffs was much quarried for Portland Stone in the nineteenth and early twentieth centuries while inland it was the more decorative Purbeck Stone that was, and still is, worked. To the north of the coast, parallel to the two limestones, lies the Chalk ridge, a narrow line because here the Chalk layers lie steeply dipping. This natural barrier is punctuated by two gaps, in one of which lies the famous castle of Corfe.

Corfe Castle

Corfe Castle has a history to match any such fortification; it was first developed by the Saxons and the castle hill provided a natural defensive position to block the way of marauding Viking raiders. It was here in 978 AD that the young King Edward was murdered, probably on the orders of his stepmother Aelfthryth. He had stopped to call in on Aelfthryth after a day out hunting and legend has it that he was handed a cup of wine before dismounting, then stabbed and his body thrown down a well. His body was later recovered and taken first to Wareham and finally Shaftesbury. Edward was the son and heir to King Edgar who had presided over a golden age of Anglo-Saxon England and Aelfthryth had wanted her son Ethelred to be king. He was duly crowned and became known to history as "the Unready". Ethelred is usually regarded as a weak king, forced by the Vikings to pay huge sums in "Danegeld". However, it may not have been much better had Edward lived, despite his later veneration as a saint, in his youth he was renowned for a violent temper and was not popular.

Corfe Castle

Above: The 'Golden Bowl', part of the Encombe Estate.

In 1138 the castle was unsuccessfully besieged by King Stephen in the civil war with Matilda, the daughter of Henry I. Corfe was greatly enlarged and improved by the Normans and was a stronghold much favoured by King John. It was here that he imprisoned Eleanor the "Fair Maid of Britanny" because she had a legitimate claim to the throne. Eleanor was the daughter of John's older brother Geoffrey and she died at Corfe in 1241. William de Braose was a supporter of John who had helped 'take care' of Eleanor's brother Arthur; when William fell out of favour his wife and child were stoned to death in Corfe Castle. Corfe's bloody history finally ended in 1646 when it was slighted by the Parliamentarians (see page 19).

Purbeck's estates

Tucked away in Purbeck's beautiful countryside are a number of fine houses, some still with considerable estates attached. The deserted village of Tyneham, requisitioned in 1944 by the army once had a lovely Elizabethan manor, now derelict. The tragic tale of this village is told in my book *The Tyneham Story*. One estate still very much thriving is Encombe, in the 'Golden Bowl' near Kingston. John Scott, the first Earl of Eldon, and owner of Encombe, was born in Love Lane in Newcastle in 1751. He went to grammar school and gained a scholarship to Oxford. He then obtained a fellowship but only if he remained single. John met Bessie Surtees, the beautiful daughter of a rich banker, and the pair fell in love. Neither set of parents wanted them to marry but John kidnapped Bessie and they were married in Scotland. The parents relented and they soon had a more fitting ceremony. He resumed his law studies and after making his fortune they came to Encombe. He believed to his dying day that Bessie was the most perfect woman.

Neighbouring Encombe is the Smedmore estate at Kimmeridge. After the Norman conquest the estate was owned by Cerne Abbey and the Smedmore family. John Clavell purchased the Cerne Abbey holding and Kimmeridge at the Dissolution of the Monasteries in 1539. The Mansels married into the Clavell family in 1830 and in World War I two daughters of the house, Marcia and Juliet, went to serve as nurses on the Western Front, first with the British and then the French Red Cross as the French Red Cross were nearer the front lines and they felt it would be more challenging. Both sisters won the Croix de Guerre. Juliet had married in 1910 but her husband was killed in 1914. She later married a French officer and settled in France. In World War II Marcia again nursed the troops and received a second Croix de Guerre. Marcia never married but took up acting and was a teacher at RADA. They wrote many letters home which are on display in Smedmore House.

In 1540 two Purbeck estates, Steeple and Creech Grange, were bought by Sir Oliver Lawrence. His family had intermarried with the Washington family in the fourteenth century. In 1657 John Washington from the family settled in America and it was his great grandson who became the first president. If you visit the beautiful, isolated church at Steeple near Kimmeridge you will see, in the porch, the coat of arms of the Washington family carved on the wall. Part of the design are stars and stripes and it is said that when George Washington was seeking inspiration for the American flag he found it on his signet ring.

Below: The Italianate church at Kingston, endowed by John Scott.

Above: Looking across the Smedmore estate to Kimmeridge from Swyre Head.

A Dorset soldier

To conclude our tales from the Isle of Purbeck we should visit the ancient church at Studland, parts of which date from Saxon times and was founded by St Aldhelm. Studland has a long, dramatic and often violent history; Viking raiders, medieval pirates and more recent smugglers have all found its sheltered bay and gently sloping beaches to their advantage. Near the entrance to the church is the grave of a soldier who came to Studland for what it now is, a place of beauty and tranquility. Serjeant William Lawrence was a veteran of the Napoleonic wars and his headstone tells a remarkable story. He fought in all of the major battles of the Peninsular campaign, being badly wounded at Badajoz after volunteering for the 'Forlorn Hope' (the group who first stormed the defences). His last battle was Waterloo and afterwards, while still in France, he met and married a French girl who he brought back to England. They lived happily at Studland for many years as keepers of the local pub (now the Bankes Arms). William recorded his adventures in a book – *A Dorset Soldier.*

Above: The grave of Sgt. Lawrence.

Thomas Hardy

Thomas Hardy was born on June 2nd 1840 at Higher Bockhampton near Dorchester. The secluded cottage is now owned by the National Trust and is open to visitors. It was here in 1874 that he wrote the novel that was to propel him to fame – *Far From the Madding Crowd.* At sixteen Hardy was apprenticed to a Dorchester firm of architects and worked on a number of churches around the county. He concentrated on his writing after the success of *Far From the Madding Crowd* and after a short stay at Sturminster Newton and then London, Hardy moved into Max Gate, a home he had designed himself on the outskirts of Dorchester. This, too, is owned by the National Trust and open to visitors. It was at Max Gate that Hardy wrote four of his most famous novels, *The Mayor of Casterbridge, The Woodlanders, Tess of the D'Ubervilles* and *Jude the Obscure.* The last of these caused such public outrage that, in 1885, Hardy gave up writing novels and from then on concentrated on poetry until his death in 1928.

As well as his cottage and Max Gate there are a number of places in and around Dorchester with Hardy associations. The Dorset County Museum has a replica of his study at Max Gate and a section devoted to the author. A short stroll from the museum is Dorchester prison and it was here that Hardy first witnessed a public hanging, the execution of Elizabeth

Above: Hardy's cottage at Higher Bockhampton.

Martha Brown in 1856. Only sixteen at the time, the event left a lasting impression on the author and perhaps provided inspiration for the end of the eponymous heroine in *Tess of the D'Urbervilles*. Also nearby is a small, thatched dwelling called 'Hangman's Cottage', once the home of the prison's own hangman.

Athelhampton, in the nearby village of Puddletown, is a delightful fifteenth century manor house at which Thomas Hardy was a regular visitor, often coming with his father who was a stonemason and worked on the house. Hardy was dining at the house in 1914 when it was announced that Britain was at war with Germany.

Thomas Hardy's heart is buried in the small churchyard at Stinsford, not far from the cottage in which he was born (his ashes were interred in Poet's Corner in Westminster Abbey). Alongside him are his two wives and parents. His father used to play violin in the gallery of the church when Hardy was a boy and the decline of this tradition is lamented in *Under the Greenwood Tree.*

Above: Athelhampton House.
Right: Hangman's Cottage in Dorchester.

Poole

Many locals have no doubt told visitors to Poole that they have arrived at the second largest natural harbour in the world (after Sydney). Formed at the end of the last Ice Age by a rise in sea level that drowned the valley of the Solent River, Poole Harbour has been an important port since the Iron Age. A longboat dating from around 300 BC was found in the harbour and is now in Poole Museum. The Roman general and future emperor Vespasian founded a port facility at Hamworthy and later on Viking raiders found the harbour an ideal base. It is thought the town of Poole was founded in the twelfth century after Wareham was burned during a siege in the civil war between King Stephen and Matilda.

In the early eighteenth century the merchants of Poole became very wealthy thanks to the trade with North America and the fishing industry off Newfoundland; Poole's ships brought huge quantities of fish back to the Catholic countries of Europe. The geology around Poole consists largely of the relatively recent sands, gravels and clays of the Wareham Basin. These deposits were laid down by a great river bringing sediment from newly eroded granite uplands in Devon. One of these layers, Purbeck Ball Clay has been used for centuries to make pottery but large scale extraction began in the eighteenth century. Josiah Wedgwood used great quantities of it as did Carters Tiles, a Poole business started in Victorian times that later became the world famous Poole Pottery. Most of the tiles that line London's underground stations were manufactured by Carters.

Poole Harbour

Above: The seventeenth century packhorse bridge in Tarrant Launceston.

The Tarrants

A number of pretty villages lie along the course of the charming River Tarrant, each with a colourful history. The river is a twelve mile long tributary of the River Stour and its name derives from the Celtic word for trespasser, for in winter the little river frequently overflows its channel and 'trespasses' over the surrounding countryside. Eight villages line this delightful valley, each having a name beginning "Tarrant". The area has a long and fascinating history stretching back to ancient times.

A grand mansion

Tarrant Gunville sits at the head of the valley near the source of the river and once contained one of the largest and grandest stately homes in all of England. Designed by John Vanbrugh on the instructions of George Doddington, Lord of the Admiralty, Eastbury House would eventually rival Blenheim and Castle Howard. It was started in 1718 but in 1720 Doddington died leaving his estate to his nephew George Bubb. Bubb-Doddington, as he became known, was determined to finish the project and by 1738 was the owner of a fabulous stately home. A vain, ambitious and corpulent man, he was something of a dandy and a member of the notorious "Hellfire Club" whose hedonistic activities were the subject of many rumours. George Bubb-Doddington died in 1762 and the estate was sold to Richard, Earl Temple who in turn left it to his son, the second Earl Temple. The second earl found the house too expensive to maintain and while living in Italy for health reasons left instructions for his steward, William Doggett to supervise the dismantling of parts of the house and the sale of materials. Doggett did not expect his master to return and arranged for the main part of the house to be dismantled as well, pocketing the money for himself. When Earl Temple arrived unexpectedly Doggett realised the futility of trying to conceal what he had done and went into the house and shot himself. This tragic story gave rise to a legend that the ghost of Doggett can sometimes be seen arriving at Eastbury on a coach driven by a headless coachman; Doggett enters the house and re-enacts his suicide.

Tarrant Gunville was the home for a time of Josiah Wedgwood II, son of the famous potter. Their business obtained much clay from the area and Josiah's brother, Thomas lived at the diminished Eastbury House from 1800 but sadly died there in 1805 at the age of thirty-four. Thomas was one of the pioneers of photography and was the first person to make an image using silver nitrate.

Tarrant Rushton was home to a key airfield in World War II and was the base for gliders which took elite forces on missions behind enemy lines (see page 45).

Below: The decaying main gateway of the once mighty Eastbury House.

Above: What remains of Eastbury House is still an impressive residence.

A gold coffin

At Tarrant Crawford the abbey, founded in the twelfth century, was once the most prosperous Cistercian nunnery in England. All that remains of the abbey is the church, now the parish church of St Mary. In the graveyard is said to be the body of Queen Joan of Scotland, buried in a gold coffin. Joan was the daughter of King John and was married to King Alexander of Scotland at the age of ten; she died when she was twenty seven in 1238. Inside the church are some very well preserved medieval wall paintings from the thirteenth and fourteenth centuries.

Below: The church of St Mary at Tarrant Crawford.

The Swing Riots and the Tolpuddle Martyrs

Between 1604 and 1914 more than five thousand Enclosure Acts meant that 6.8 million acres of land was enclosed. Much of this had been common land that peasants and farm labourers had been able to use for grazing animals and growing vegetables. Wealthy landowners increasingly wanted to farm more efficiently and to make more money from the rents paid by tenants. The beginning of the nineteenth century saw the introduction of new farm machinery, in particular threshing machines that were much more efficient than human labour. Threshing usually went on from November to January and provided much work for labourers. All this 'progress' had a devastating effect on the rural poor; there was less work available, lower wages and successive Enclosure Bills had deprived them of a means of growing their own food. Then in 1829 and 1830 two successive poor harvests led to widespread unrest and riots spread across the south of England.

Threatening letters were sent to farmers and landowners in the name of "Captain Swing", almost certainly an entirely fictitious character, warning them of dire consequences if they didn't raise wages and/or get rid of new machinery that was deemed to be depriving labourers of work. At first many farmers capitulated but later the authorities began to take a firm stance and the militia was used to suppress riots. The riots started in Kent and quickly spread across the south of England. On 23rd November 1830 there were riots in Cranborne and Edmonsham and on 26th November rioters from Mappowder in north Dorset destroyed a threshing machine. The government acted swiftly and ruthlessly. In January 1831 a special court was set up at Dorchester where fifty-seven men awaited trial. Eventually twelve Dorset men were transported to Australia.

An incident in Puddletown may have involved men who were later to play a part in the story of the Tolpuddle Martyrs. The plight of farm labourers in Dorset was especially desperate. The Chalk downlands did not provide rich farmland and the contrast with the neighbouring vales in Somerset and their prosperous dairies gave rise to the phrase "chalk and cheese" to symbolise this. In Tolpuddle a man named George Loveless was among the farm labourers earning nine shillings a week and living in poverty. In 1834 he decided to form a union to give the labourers more bargaining power. George and five others met under the tree on the green in Tolpuddle, reputedly swearing an oath of secrecy. What they did was not illegal, but the local squire James Frampton was determined to suppress any signs of rebellion. He began gathering evidence and the six men were

Above: The Vale of Blackmore from the Chalk landscape of Cranborne Chase - "chalk and cheese".
Right: The Martyrs' Shelter at Tolpuddle built in 1934. To the right is the sycamore, which experts have confirmed is old enough for the martyrs to have met under its spreading branches.

eventually brought to trial on a trumped up charge of swearing an illegal oath. Frampton and several of his family and associates sat on the jury and the men were duly sentenced to transportation, a fearful punishment that many did not survive.

News of their sentence spread and the newly formed trade union movement began to organise protests. In April 1834 a huge demonstration involving up to one hundred thousand people took place in London and sympathetic MPs repeatedly raised the issue in Parliament. The government was finally forced to pardon the men and in Spring 1836 the men were on their way home. George Loveless returned to Tolpuddle but, not finding the situation much improved, emigrated to Canada with four of the other Martyrs where he became a farmer and helped set up a Methodist church. Only one of the original six, James Hammett, stayed in Tolpuddle where he worked as a builder's labourer.

Tolpuddle is still remembered as the birthplace of the Trade Union movement and every July thousands come for the annual festival and rally.

Cranborne

Cranborne Chase was a royal hunting ground from the time of William the Conqueror to the early nineteenth century. Monarchs later bestowed or sold the franchise to keep deer to local landowners. The Chase was a favourite hunting ground of King John who is known to have hunted here at least fourteen times. Today it is a beautiful and peaceful landscape but in the eighteenth century it was anything but. Deer, protected by law for the aristocratic hunters, were the cause of bloody encounters between poachers and gamekeepers. Farmers struggled to protect their crops from the deer, but harsh punishments awaited any caught harming them. The Chase was also criss-crossed by paths used by smugglers to transport their contraband inland from the coast; all in all it could be a wild and lawless place at times.

Cranborne itself was once an important administrative centre for the Chase, soldiers were garrisoned here and the manor was the site of King John's hunting lodge. A number of kings came here to hunt including Henry VIII and James I. The lodge was acquired by Robert Cecil, First Minister to Elizabeth I and James II, in 1604 and he remodelled it into what is now Cranborne Manor. Cecil was the first Earl of Salisbury and the manor is now home to Viscount Cranborne, a courtesy title to the heir of the Earls of Salisbury based at Hatfield House.

Above: Cranborne - on the hill to the left stood the Norman castle.

Above and right: The lovely manor at Cranborne, built by Robert Cecil in 1604. It remains a charming family home. It is not open to the public but visitors can stroll around the beautiful gardens on Wednesdays in the summer.

There was a prosperous Saxon abbey here before the Conquest, founded in 980 by a descendant of Edward the Elder with the wonderful name of Haylward Snew who, by all accounts, was a particularly handsome man. A grandson of Haylward's called Brihtric was responsible for enlarging the abbey. He seems to have inherited his grandfather's looks and while on a diplomatic mission to Normandy had attracted the attention of Matilda, daughter of the Count of Flanders. He spurned her advances however and, unluckily for Brihtric, Matilda later married Duke William of Normandy; she did not forget the insult and later had William confiscate Brihtric's land and throw him into prison where he died.

Dorset and the First and Second World Wars

In a central position on the south coast of England, Dorset played a key part in preparations and training for the services during both world wars. Portland Harbour, in 1914, was home to the First Fleet, later to be known as the Grand Fleet. As war loomed ever closer the mighty warships in the harbour looked vulnerable to attack and the First Lord of the Admiralty, Winston Churchill, ordered that they move north to the safer waters of Scapa Flow in the Orkneys. They began this move on the evening of 29th July, without lights or radio contact. Portland would still be an important base and it was thought to be particularly vulnerable to attack via the south entrance. Here torpedo nets would not stay in place due to the strong tidal outflow so it was decided to close the entrance permanently by scuttling the old battleship HMS Hood across the entrance; she remains there to this day.

HMS Formidable

On New Year's Day 1915 the first British battleship to be sunk in the Great War was hit by two torpedoes in Lyme Bay. The 15 000 ton HMS Formidable had about 750 crew on board of whom only 233 survived. One life boat was washed up at Lyme Regis with about fifty men on board, some of them already dead and others dying. The bodies were taken to the Pilot Boat Inn where the landlord had offered the cellar as a temporary mortuary. The pub's dog, a collie cross named Lassie reputedly began to lick the face of one of the unfortunate seamen, a man named John Cowan. She persisted with this and eventually it was noticed that Cowan was moving. He was taken to hospital and made a full recovery. Some think Lassie was the inspiration for the fictional dog of that name.

View over Portland Harbour

Above: The Tyneham valley viewed from the limestone ridge to the south. This landscape provided ideal terrain for gunnery practice - shells could be fired at targets on the hillside with the sea behind for any badly aimed. The area is still the army's main artillery training facility. The village of Tyneham and the range walks are open to the public most weekends and school holidays.

Tanks

1916 saw the establishment of the Tank Corps at Bovington. The development of the tank was top secret and farmers and villagers were warned to stay indoors as the strange machines made their way along the quiet, narrow country lanes. Later the Gunnery School at Lulworth was established and much disruption was caused by tanks travelling backwards and forwards.

D-Day preparations

The story of Dorset in World War II is largely bound up in the preparations for D-Day and the subsequent Battle of Normandy. Thousands of American troops were based in the county prior to the invasion; humble village homes and grand manors were temporarily requisitioned and thousands of vehicles lined the country lanes. As said before, around half a million men embarked from Portland and Weymouth with many more from Poole. In April 1944 Studland Bay was the scene of a huge rehearsal for the Normandy landings; live ammunition was used and the proceedings were watched by Winston Churchill, King George VI and generals Eisenhower and Montgomery. They watched from the safety of Fort Henry, a specially constructed concrete observation post that still stands to this day. Studland was chosen because the area most resembled the Normandy beaches where the landings would take place.

The gunnery ranges at Lulworth were vital training areas and late in 1943 it was decided that more land was needed. The Tyneham valley on the eastern edge of the ranges was taken over which led to the evacuation of the village and neighbouring Worbarrow Bay. Despite promises to the contrary the villagers were never able to return to their homes and the ruined houses, church and school now form a picturesque memorial to country life in the early twentieth century (see also page 29).

Worth Matravers and the development of radar

There is little in and around the pretty Purbeck village of Worth Matravers to reveal its importance to the war effort in the 1940s, but it was here that important developments were made in the use of radar. Between May 1940 and May 1942 Worth was the primary centre for radar development. It was chosen because of its position near flat cliff tops from which signals could be sent out and received over long distances. Huge masts over three hundred feet tall were originally needed because of the long wavelengths involved but the scientists at Worth worked on developing radar that worked with much shorter wavelengths, enabling it to be fitted to aircraft. By 1942 around two thousand people worked there, but it was decided to move the work to the Malvern Hills because of the perceived danger of a German raid.

Below: Looking west from St Aldhelm's Head. The radar memorial and Norman chapel are a little way to the right of the photograph. This location was chosen because of the high, flat cliff tops.

Above: Tarrant Rushton airfield has largely returned to farmland, but some of the perimeter road and a hangar remain. Inset: A detail from the memorial.

There is a memorial to the development of radar on the cliffs of St Aldhelm's Head, where in August 1940 the first echoes from a radar set were received from the Norman chapel. The nearby Square and Compass pub was popular with scientists who reputedly nicknamed it the 'Sine and Cosine'. A display about the work can be found in the Swanage Museum and Heritage Centre.

Tarrant Rushton airfield

It was not only Dorset's ports that were important embarkation points for the Allied forces taking part in Operation Overlord, the invasion of Normandy in 1944. The airfield at Tarrant Rushton played a key role. On the night of 5th June 1944 gliders took off with troops whose job was to capture two bridges that later became known as Pegasus and Horsa. This was crucial to stop the Germans reinforcing their positions that would come under attack on June 6th. It is said that the first glider to land did so rather heavily and catapulted two aircrew through the front cockpit window. Bruised but not deterred, these were the first troops to land in France on D-Day. Gliders from the airfield later took soldiers to the fierce fighting at Arnhem and also took supplies to French Resistance fighters. Today the airfield has largely been returned to agricultural land but one giant hangar remains and there is a simple memorial near the roadside.

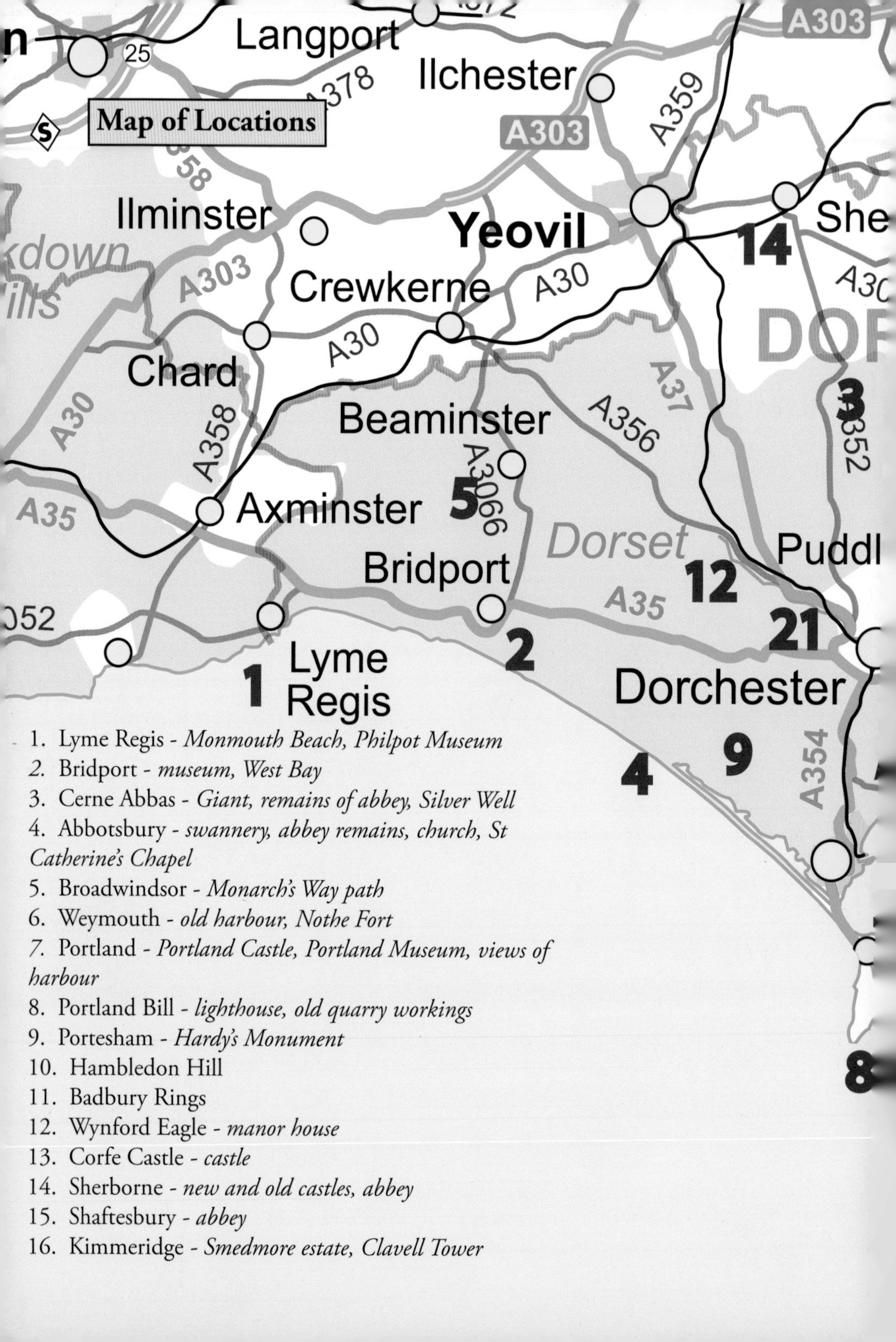

1. Lyme Regis - *Monmouth Beach, Philpot Museum*
2. Bridport - *museum, West Bay*
3. Cerne Abbas - *Giant, remains of abbey, Silver Well*
4. Abbotsbury - *swannery, abbey remains, church, St Catherine's Chapel*
5. Broadwindsor - *Monarch's Way path*
6. Weymouth - *old harbour, Nothe Fort*
7. Portland - *Portland Castle, Portland Museum, views of harbour*
8. Portland Bill - *lighthouse, old quarry workings*
9. Portesham - *Hardy's Monument*
10. Hambledon Hill
11. Badbury Rings
12. Wynford Eagle - *manor house*
13. Corfe Castle - *castle*
14. Sherborne - *new and old castles, abbey*
15. Shaftesbury - *abbey*
16. Kimmeridge - *Smedmore estate, Clavell Tower*

17. St Aldhelm's Head - *radar memorial, Norman chapel, Worth Matravers*
18. Wareham - *Saxon church and walls, quay*
19. Kingston - *church, Encombe estate*
20. Studland - *church (grave of Sgt Lawrence), Fort Henry*
21. Dorchester - *museum, Thomas Hardy sites*
22. Puddletown - *Athelhampton House, church*
23. Milton Abbas - *abbey, school, village*
24. Poole - *quay, museum*
25. Tarrant valley - *Tarrant Rushton airfield, Eastbury House*
26. Tolpuddle - *martyrs' tree, museum*
27. Cranborne - *manor house, castle hill*

Bibliography and Further Reading

The Escape of Charles II after the Battle of Worcester - Richard Ollard, Constable and Robinson, 2002

Dorset in the English Civil War - Robert Morris, Stuart Press, 1995

The Dorset Village Book - Harry and Hugh Ashley, Countryside Books, 2000

The Dorset Coast, History, Lore and Legend - Harry Ashley, Countryside Books, 2000

A Tour Through the Whole Island of Great Britain - Daniel Defoe, edited by Pat Rogers, The Promotional Reprint Company Ltd., 1989

Ancient Dorset (2nd Ed.)- Robert Westwood, Inspiring Places Publishing, 2015

Dark Age Dorset - Robert Westwood, Inspiring Places Publishing, 2007

Tales of the Dorset Coast - Robert Hesketh, Inspiring Places Publishing, 2015

Legends and Folklore of Dorset - Robert Hesketh, Inspiring Places Publishing, 2014

A Dorset Soldier - William Lawrence, edited by Eileen Hathaway, The History Press Ltd., 1995

Front cover: Milton Abbey from St Catherine's Chapel.

Rear cover: The bridge at Lower Bockhampton.

Title page background: Athelhampton House.

This page background: "Old" Sherborne Castle.

All photographs by the author except page 39 (smaller photo) by Robert Hesketh.